Augusta Kautz

A World My Own

Augusta Kautz

A World My Own

ISBN/EAN: 9783743303706

Manufactured in Europe, USA, Canada, Australia, Japa

Cover: Foto ©Suzi / pixelio.de

Manufactured and distributed by brebook publishing software
(www.brebook.com)

Augusta Kautz

A World My Own

A WORLD MY OWN.

DEDICATED TO

" The friends who love me,
The friends I know are true,
The heaven that shines above me,
And waits my spirit too."

Anon.

BY THE AUTHOR,

AUGUSTA KAUTZ.

———

PRESS OF
H. S. CROCKER COMPANY,
SAN FRANCISCO.
1896.

"When the world is dark and cold in seeming,
   And friends I love have changed or flown,
I wander away in spirit, dreaming
   Of light and beauty in a world my own."
                                    Anon.

INDEX..

✦

"We Musicians Know."

Browning.

THE poet, who with mortal eyes
   Sees past cerulean distance,
Would bring to earth those bending skies
   To brighten earth existence ;
But fails to snare the soul's lost words,
   And, lacking that assistance,
His speech, for songs of skyey birds,
   Derides by its resistance.

5

Ethereal Messengers.

OH, hush! Do not say that to beautify thought
    I seek, in my poor little rhymes;
True thought is the soul of the universe, wrought
    Too subtile for my jangling chimes;
But out from its bounty holy whispers are kept
    Afloat, like sweet incense away; —
And I only seek to their route intercept,
    To rehearse what the messengers say.

So subtile their meanings, my gross finite sense
    Can never quite understand.
Heaven's wayfaring guests, they are journeying whence
    Some song-loving poet shall stand,
Rehearsing in song those strains of the skies,
    Which never shall echo again ;
For songs so intense but echo in cries
    The throes of a sanctified pain.

6

Irresponsive.

YOU say I shall sing you a word-song,
    A melody, to impart
The joyous thrill of a bird-song
    To a sobbing, broken heart.
I have listened to the birds and the breezes,
    My pen at my finger tips;
Not a chord in all their music
    Will spring to my pen or my lips.

Then how can I tune my dumb lyre
    To sounds I myself do not know?
Once my heart sang the songs you desire,
    But that was a long time ago.
There never was song worth the singing,
    But rang from a soul's overflow;
But what sets the measures a-ringing,
    No one shall ever know.

Whe good our Father still to bless
Th midnight prairie wilderness.

Midnight on the Prairie.

WRITTEN IN 1869.

'TIS midnight on the prairie.
   Methinks if I had angel wings,
     To soar to yonder star,
   The silence there would be less still
     Than midnights on the prairies are.

Above, around, is solitude,
   Fresh from the Maker's hand,—
Repose as pure as Paradise
   Ere sin was in the land.
The dew-tears on that bud are pure,
   Not wept o'er sin or shame;
Those flowers hide no cruel grave,
   For here death never came.

The moonlight falls with reverence there,
   As if 'twere holy shrine;
The hush is like the hush of prayer
   Of angel's evening time.

S

The starlight shimmers on the scene,
    Where hallowed, voiceless air,
So dreamy, peaceful and serene,
    Seems answering angels' prayer,
Who plead our Father still to bless
The midnight prairie wilderness.

Unity.

♣

THE tide of the universe throbs in me,—
    A pulsing current strong;
My great-heart-beats for a higher life
    Are timed with Nature's song.
The ardor of my upward strife
    Will bloom in the yet-to-be.

A Prairie Scene.

WRITTEN IN 1870.

♣

IN the Prairie's still hush,
   Where the wild-flowers blush,
And stars watch the stillness so deep,
    Is the grave of a stranger,
    Of a brave Texas ranger,
But no friend ever goes there to weep.

   Perfumed breezes caress
   Blooms no footstep shall press
On that prairie, the "Garden of God;"
    For no guests ever wander
    To the grave over yonder,
Where so sadly the green grasses nod.

   There the wild-flowers twine
   A sepulchral vine,
That nods to the darkness around ;
    And the night-wind's low whisper
    Wakes but fairies to list her,
While she sings a low dirge o'er the mound.

10

Is it fancy makes seem,
Like the shade of a dream?
Or do serpents' huge arms hug the clods?
Or when storms march to battle,
And the rains meet to prattle,
Do I hear mournful wails o'er the sods?

　　*　　　*　　　*　　　*

Oh! The shadows fall dark
On some hearth, where they hark
For a step they shall nevermore hear!
Little think he is sleeping
Where the hushed hours are keeping
Lonely vigils of grief all the year.

　　*　　　*　　　*　　　*

Little think the boatman, pale,
Hung his oar,—reefed his sail,—
Till life's chain slowly loosed captive bands,—
Freed a soul for its Giver,
To be borne o'er the river,
To rejoice in the bright summer lands.

11

My Soul.

OH, Life! Oh, Soul!
Invisible river! roll,
And seek unseen, that unseen sea,—
                    Immensity!

Thou soundless song!
Oh, roll, dream-voice, along!
Thou note of the Universe! Of it be
                    Part Harmony.

Oh, unseen Giver,
Unite this unseen river
To that strange, unseen, tideless sea,—
                    Eternity!

Pass by earth's shore,
Thou unseen breeze! Oh, soar
Past heaven's verge! Thy flight shall be
                    Infinity.

Oh, child divine,
Heaven's grandeur is thine,
To tread the march of Time's rehearse
                    Of the Universe.

I Wonder.

HOW strangely hues of childhood mingle
  With threadbare cares of years,—
Like sunbeams spun of sheeny splendor,
  All woven in with tears;
Like silvery warp with woof of ashes;
  Like moonbeams knit with clouds;
Night tangled tight with lightning's tresses,
  Bright angels clothed in shrouds.

Will this life mock the life up yonder
  By mingling with its flow?
Or will it be a life, I wonder,
  Unedged by hems of woe?
Life's bitterness be quite forgot,—
  Forgot its loves and bains?
Or memory, like immortal shadows,
  Belink our joys and pains.

13

Has heaven's portal higher threshold
    Than reach our neighbor's door?
Is heaven aught but " inner kingdom
    Within us,"—nothing more ?
If joys, and tears, and sins forgot,
    Then self's forgotten, too,
Annihilating us completely
    As atheists could do.

The Seeking Soul.

FOR there are times when earthly headlands high
    Encroach upon the threshold of the sky,
And heaven and earth unite in holy place,
And spirit earthy and divine embrace.
The crystal sea shall cleanse earth's turbid main,
If human hate in arms of love is slain ;
For love reborn—our inner priesthood shrives,
And earth and heaven mingle in our lives.

Air Castles.

NO life is so meager, so sad, or so empty,
   But o'er it some brightness has shone.
It has known all the bliss of a youth's early dreaming,
   With that magical beauty,—its own.

The castle then built had no airy-like seeming
   When we tripped through its halls, all alone,
And planned no less bliss down life's arches was beaming,
   Than o'er all those corridors shone.

I love yet to linger by its tumble-down portal,
   And rehearse the bright visions it hid.
I reverence that memory so bright and immortal,
   If pilgrim to shrine ever did.

Though life gives us more of its nettles than roses,
   And life's failures have brought so much woe,
Yet I think we all find life's best gift still reposes
   In the old tumbled-down long ago.

Easter Morning.

♣

THAT power which keeps, through winter storms,
    Bright blossoms of blue and gold,
Placed gems more rare, in human forms,
    Kept safe 'neath life's dank mold.

Each violet's birth is no new wrought gift :
    Its germ is the Infinite's thought,—
Their safety beneath winter's downy drift,
    With infinite meaning fraught.

Each soul has its nights, and wintery drifts,
    Its springtime it has as well,
Its Easter morn, when it skyward lifts,
    And blooms like the asphodel.

My Last Request.

♣

I ONLY ask, when life's last evening dips
    Its lamp in the western sea,—
Ere its flickering ray down the darkness slips,—
    A light in the East I see.

16

The Soul.

WHAT discovers our soul when in upward flight
   We reach for our heart's ideal,
Which ever keeps calling by day and night,—
   Yet so lofty it fails to reveal
Its beautiful face to our soul alight
   'Mong debris of the lowly real.
If by wearisome flight, we shall seek its height,
   It, ascending, escapes our zeal,—
Thus keeping our soul to the arduous fate
   Of continuous upward eyre,
Like a lone weary bird that is seeking its mate
   Up a mountain's upward stair.

Oh! mystery vaster, profounder ever,—
   My ideal, my soul, and me.
Life's meaning is truly a ceaseless endeavor
   To unite this triune three.

Life's Problem.

❧

WE oft in life like sailors stand,
    On deck in stormy seas.
  From up on high, in accents grand,
      A stranger voice is calling :
"Go search life's black sky's meaning out,
    Its secret understand !
  With naught but seething waves about,
    And far away from land,
      Hear not ye voices calling ? "

  Life's surges roll ; we beat about
    Upon life's tumbling tide.
We drift, and drift, and drifting out,
    Aloft rings out the warning :
Go search ! Nor linger, plead, or ask !
    Interpret life yet more !
'Tis late to learn life's cruel task
    When cast upon its shore
      On that supernal morning.

So oft does awe and mystery blend
    Quite to life's bending edge.
When loved ones leap, where pathways end,
    Down depths of awful silence,
We call, and call. The depths are dumb ;
    No answer comes below.
Life has its envoy ; Death has none
    Except its awful silence.

The White Lily by Moonlight.

THOU sprite of the vale ! Thou moonlight's bride !
    In bridal robes of white.
Thou angel bright, of wings denied,
    Berobed in lustrous light !
Thou white-robed nun, so soulful sweet,
    Moonbeams you glorified !
Or art thou spirit, whose winding sheet
    The grave has scintillized ?

The Spiritually Learned.

THE storm may shake the clouds in its grasp,
 The welkin's thunders roar;
Still stars shine on at their wonted task,
 As calmly as heretofore.

As stars shine on, though the night be dark,
 And gems 'neath gowns of sands,
So the deathless soul, that living spark,
 All darksome depths withstands.

The clouds shall seek their ocean crypt,
 And splash in the breakers' brine;
With immortal burnish, stars are tipped,
 And shall forever shine.

Who knows no sin his soul shall dim
 Knows what soul treasures be.
He knows their sheen is God in him,—
 And immortality.

Soul Tethered to the Body.

POOR soul! Meek captive! Dost heed thy bitter fate?
Fast bound to one lone comrade, not genial mate,
One, coarse by nature,—not fellow, nor yet friend,—
And thou, to guide that wretch, and guard him to the end?
For long thy captor may hold his captive bound,
Thy counsel scorned, thy low voice in coarse jest drowned.
Poor soul! Held fast in close embracing arms of clod;—
And thou, the much loved child of most High God!
When midnight's hushed repose has curtained off the day,
And deathlike slumber has bound thy charge of clay,
Then yearn'st thou not for Father, and for Father's home?
Why shun'st thou, then, the path which spans the space-
    ful gloam?
Thou child—immortal! Whatever can it be
So links my mortal part with thy eternity?

Unsatisfied.

What does it signify
That life ne'er rounds to full completeness,
Nor joys attain an unmixed sweetness,
    And pleasures ever flee
    With strangest fleetness,
And quite brimful nothing ever seems to be?

    And sorrows multiply.
Experience bringing grief unending,
Yet never quite affects a mending
    Of ills which fill life's day,
    Despite the recommending
That knowledge bought by years is better every way.

    Will nothing satisfy?
Will souls, this side of life's fulfillment,
Be taught by tasks of life's instillment,
    And ever come to know
    The sweet enthrillment
Of knowing all the meaning of our life's work here below?

22

Somehow.

♣

I FEEL to-day at life's edge I wait
For Death to open the border gate.
I know not why,—I have felt alway,—
That I, not Death, would court delay.
I ne'er till now felt my life work o'er,
But hoped, somehow, to accomplish more.
To-day, in counting of all I've wrought,
On each white page I found,—but naught.

I hoped I'd heritage wondrous fair,
That I was one to earth's glory heir.
I sought it well,—nor in lowly place;
I gazed aloft for its heaven-lit face;
I felt, somehow, it was pure and vast,—
Though not of earth, yet of earthy cast,—

A gem not given to deck my brow,
But one whose lustre would cheer, somehow,
Poor human hearts when faint with woe,
As the sun bends backward its gorgeous glow

23

Of ruffly gilt to be-edge the night,
And dot it over with specks of light.
My dream, somehow, must have played me false:
I missed my path in my life's mad waltz.
Was I too earthy ? Or hopes too high ?
I never reached where the jewels lie.
Or were my eyes so dimmed by tears,
I missed possession all these years ?
No matter now; the hour grows late;
Haste, Death, and open the border gate!

Too Late.

OH, Time, unloose the clasp of thy painful hand !
Up yonder path we came together.
I must return and touch my childhood's hand,
And say, " Farewell, farewell, forever!"

Life's Song.

OH! could I all things wrong surrender,
With ardor seek celestial splendor,
My love for Him a yearning be,
As yearns the rill for the mighty sea, —
Which bears upon its tuneful tide
Sweet music for the world beside ; —
If life bore plans, and words, and deeds,
Befitting all of human needs,
Life's current set to sweetest tunes,
Kept true Decembers, as in Junes,
My life—like music of the rills,
Which ocean's depths keeps singing still—
A song immortal then would be,
A river's song in a soundful sea. .

October.

✤

OCTOBER is here,
The best of the year,
  I know by this display.
She rifled the bow
Of beatific glow
  To deck her own array ;
Bespangled the green,
With bright leaves between,
  Then added a sprinkle of gray ;
Hung a bright golden sheen,
With the apple leaves green,
  And purple along the vines' way.
O'er the brown, tangled weeds,
And the beautiful reeds,
  She scattered a soft, silvery spray,
Which the sunshine bright
Beglitters with light,
  Like diamond aurora.
Even painted at eve
The clouds that wreathe
  The ramparts of retreating day.

The First Frost of Autumn.

NOVEMBER, fleeing, frowned in anger,
  And drew her drapery tight.
Chill breezes whispered low, in languor,
  November's last good-night.
The frost gleamed white, in sheeny splendor,
  On flower, leaf and tree ;
For silvery moonlight, cool and tender,
  Walked o'er the gem-lit lea.
Its silvery woof with frost warp mingles
  Its weaving left and right,—
O'er leafy dells and drowzy dingles
  Spreads blankets dazzling white.
The North King sends his Arctic tribute,—
  Boreas' icy car,
Well lade with jewels for December
  To scatter near and far.

The Rivals.

♣

FROM out October's ruddy car
　　Stepped stately, cold November,—
A princess from the cold North star,
　　With a retinue of splendor.
December scorned the icy pride
　　Of the haughty Northern princess.
He tallied time for Christmas tide,
　　And called his hoary ministress.
She strode Boreas' steed to ride,
　　And lassoed Arctic splendor
　　　　Of ermine clouds,—in white to hide
The luster of November.

"Night Bringeth All Things Home."

♣

LIFE'S evening bringeth us all to our home.
　No sunset shall gild that heavenly dome.
The fervor of sunrise shall be its adorning.
'T will not be our evening, but be morning.

Farewell, Darling.

❦

LIFE'S glamour is faded, life's hopes rudely broken ;
And compelled, at the last, these sad words have been spoken,—
Farewell, darling, my dearest!
Ah! little we thought in our love's sunny Maytime,
When we thought of each other, by night-time, and daytime,
To say, ever say, Farewell, darling, my dearest!

How could we have thought, when so happy together,
We, compelled, would speak words that would ring out forever,—
Farewell, darling, my dearest!
Can my heart e'er be taught that it faints not, or calls not ?
Can my hands press my ears, that your dear accent falls not ?
That calls, ever calls, Farewell, darling, my dearest?

Will your words, like a ghost-song, forever come thither ?
Will they come, on each breeze, with such pleadings that quiver ?
Farewell, darling, my dearest!
When our love is consumed on love's own strange built altar,
Then our hearts will they cry not, or lips pale not, nor falter
To say, sadly say, Farewell, darling, my dearest!

I ween darkened halls of my heart will be guestless;
Night and day they will echo than the sea waves more restless,—
Farewell, darling, my dearest!
It is said that each bosom some sepulcher closes,
That some weed will grow green on the bed of dead roses,
But naught can replace my lost darling, my dearest!

Perhaps in life's flow my heart's cry shall be stifled,
And my heart cease to cry out, that it has been rifled.
Farewell, darling, my dearest.
The thorns were all spared, but my roses were taken,
Hushed each song, save the wind's mocking cry—love forsaken!
And cries, ever cries, Farewell, darling, my dearest!

Though I olden by a wild laugh, and a still wilder weeping,
Though I mutter again, and again, when I am sleeping,—
Farewell, darling, my dearest!
Though my lips may grow pale, and my pale brow more whitened,
Though my mad lips may whisper, with maddened eyes brightened,
They will say, Thou, my darling, art dearest!

Pangs of anguish once borne, the green grave never covers.
Phantom bells will forever ring the knell of the lovers.
Farewell, darling, my dearest!

And methinks that the wild winds, in fierce, fitful blowing,
Though sepulchral vines above me be growing,
    Will shriek, wildly shriek, Farewell, darling, my dearest !

Inconstancy.

♣

THE morning's golden glories meet
    The mountain tops to flatter,
Then kiss the flowers at their feet.
    Was morn sincere ?   No matter!
For mountains bade the clouds to ride
    Upon their ragged pillows,
Then thrust them down, in wrath,—to bide
    Among the sheltering willows.

The Mountain Storm.

♣

THE clouds climbed after each other up the mountains high,
Then strode across the fenceless desert of the sky.
The raindrops fell like scattered grain of the husbandman.
The mountain torrents shouted the gale, then onward ran.

The lightning, like hissing serpents' tongues of flame,
Scourged the huge rocks, that thundered downward, rent in twain.
The writhing pine trees palavered to the angry wind.
The bellowing thunder all the mountain valleys dinned.

The timid moon, with cloudy mantles about her rolled,
Was safely hidden in their bedraggled draperies' fold.
And only the mountains stood mute, and knew no angry thrill;
While fiercely raged the tempest, they stood statelily and still.

After Many Years.

I MUSED with awe where mountain gloom
Filled crannied nook and rocky coombe.
Huge rocks like monsters of the holm
Came weirdly out the gathering gloam.
Dark shadows peeped, then forward crept,
Like drowsy gnomes who long had slept.
Then one by one the stars were tipped
With sacred fires from holy crypt.
Soft breezes crept like living things,
That seemed the sound of rustling wings.

A stream dashed madly down the fell.
All cast o'er me a magic spell.
My life, spread broad in fabric, lay
A dismal, dark and dingy gray.
And this was to my hearing brought:
"I gave good woof, but this you wrought,—
A worthless weft.   Your warp is spent,
Your shuttles empty, spindles bent."

Oh, pity, Father ! then I cried ;
To weave *this* pattern sweet I tried.
I toiled, and toiled, and I am sure
My pattern was quite spotless, pure.
This rag to dark oblivion leave,
And bless that which I meant to weave.

Your gifts were all of silvery thread,
But what I wove seems gray instead.
'Mid dust and sand for years I spun,
And meant to weave a charming one ;
But earthly strife, which soiled my hands,
Has tarnished all the lovely strands.

Beauty.

♣

IF thoughts kept pure expanded white,
   In deeds of blossomed beauty,
No misty haze, but radiant light,
   Would mark our path of duty.

Sunset in the Mountains.

♣

ALL flushed, the face of the mountains reach
    For caresses of its lover,
And pillows its head on the sky's fond breast,
    As he ardently bends over.
The weary day shuts the outer door,
    Draws curtains of purply billows.
And firefly lamps, a blazing score,
    Light up the tangled willows.

The moon dives deep into cloudy seas,
    And drowns her radiant splendor.
The pine trees nod to the hoyden breeze,
    Which kisses them so tender.
The cricket calls to its dusky mate.
    Stars shrink into misty caverns.
The frogs carouse both early and late
    In Nature's wayside taverns.

The Mountain's Midnight Gloom.

♣

I

DOWN steepest cliffs and rocky cañons,
  What dismal shadows fall.
Each tree's dark shade appears the yawning
  Of some wide cavern's wall.
Uncanny rocks seem mountain monsters
  Beside broad burrowed halls.
The coyote's howl suggests as meaning
  A ghoul's or goblin's cry.
The pain-wrenched pine trees shriek and quiver,
  As mad winds trample by.
Few stars above the scene are scattered
  Like owlets in the sky.
The moon seems, even too, to falter,
  'Where breastworks tower high.

II

Anon comes strangest, stillest silence,
  As if all Nature knelt ;

36

And angels bowed in reverent feeling,
  Such awe has Nature felt.
While o'er the scene a spell seemed stealing,
  As if genii dwelt
'Neath rocks, ravines and caverns' ceiling,
  And awful silence dealt,
As Influence weird, to aid revealing,
  Their mystic rites respelt.

III

Anon, the sun, in sheeny splendor,
  Bursts from his nighty tomb,
With benediction, soft and tender,
  Disperses all the gloom.
Each bud's "Good morning" sweetly uttered
  By bursting into bloom.
The wakened birds, with wings a-fluttered,
  Sing loud from rocky coombe.
All Nature smiles,—so soon forgot
  The midnight's wretched doom.

I love the gloomy ghoulish shadows,
The summits golden sunset's meadows

I Love Thee, Mountains!

♣

I LOVE thy gloomy, ghoulish shadows,
Thy summits golden, sunset's meadows,
Thy robe of clouds, with ruffly trailing,
Be-edged about with fleecy veiling.
Thy rocks seem altars, trees seem steeples.
Thy cañon aisles my fancy peoples
With trains of worshipers ascending
To grasp Jehovah's hand depending.

Archer.

♣

I CANNOT think of those little hands
As part of the dim unknown,
But worse, by far, of the satin bands,
They wear in their coffin lone.

For many years have those waxen hands
In their satiny bands held still.
Must sheaves of eons bind their bands,
Nor yet thy touch my pulses thrill?

A binding of billowy, raggedy spray,
Like the ravels edge of the ocean's mantle.

San Diego.

♣

CABRILLO sailed north from Natividad,
   Till his caravel furrowed a fallow bay.
  A sequestered realm, bare and solitaire,
For leagues upon leagues to the inland lay.
  Quivera's broad plain, or Cibola fair,
Might engraft on the stem of Eastern lands;
  But San Diego, apart like a wild beast's lair,
Was hermitical land. There a hermit city stands, —
  A hermit secure in a crescent fastness.
On the west bends the hem of a quiet bay;
  On the east rises high, hilly vastness,
Where solitude cradles in mountain gloom
  The unsingable song of an austere silence.
Far away the Pacific's wide waters boom
  A retort to the tempest's rude violence.
A binding of billowy, raggedy spray,
  Like the ravely edge of the ocean's mantle,
Whips the sands in the glee of a childish play,
  Where the waves on the westerly thresholds trample.

Round the bare mountain breasts of the Eastern rim,
  Blushing cloudlets the folds of their curtains double.
Down the swift sloping curves of the mountainous brim
  Gleams the rich golden fields of sunset's stubble.

When the Yule-tiding falls, then Boreas stops
  To peep o'er the easterly border,
His frost fingers clutching the bare mountain tops,
  While he scowls at our lowland warder.
For she, merry Summer, forever abides,
  Idly dreaming in a sea-breezy hammock;
Her empire a bower where side by side
    Grows the thistle, the rose and the shamrock.

Good-night.

♣

Life's evening falls.
I know I feel the twilight's fingers steal in mine,
And lead me with a gentle hand
Into the night,—where nightly shadows twine
Round life's shattered wrecks upon the strand.

Oh, silent night !
Embroidered stars upon thy silky darkness rest,—
The beacon lights of faith's own hand,—
To light the fleecing billows crest,
Which bears me to the Silent Land.

Oh, silent path !
That stretches far into the night, where pillowed rest
Awaits earth's weary ones, whose sleep
The Stygian's roar cannot arrest,
Though launched upon its billowy deep.

Oh, peace, be still !
He speaks, and slumber falls upon the lethced deep.
We calmly rest on the boatman's breast ;
For Death, our life's last guest, his tryst shall keep,
And smile upon our heaven-born rest.

Lake Ontario.

❧

HOW often, when the night hours linger,
    I listen for thy surging sea !
Forgot, that lullaby song must be
    Strings struck by memory's finger.
Then ring out cadence of those billows,
    And bear the long-hushed strains along ;
For naught could soothe my wakeful pillows
    Like the dear old cradle song.

I sometimes thought thy dark-blue waves
    Were but the sky's robe trailing,
With broidered hem of crested waves,
    And foam-sprayed, misty veiling,
Swung back and fore, o'er a glassy floor,
    Like graceful dancings to-and-fros;
But the trodden measures of *that* shore
    Are dear Ontario's.

My Dream.

♣

I DREAMED by a lake far away I reclined,
In a bower of myrtle where the wild roses twined.
Like meteors the hours were hurrying by;
The fires of youth burned again in my eye.
Again, by the power of fantasies led,
I built airy castles where my future should tread.
Youth tinged all that future with roseate glow,
And life had a zest but the youthful can know.
My memory to ashes had fallen away,
Forgotten life's sorrows, its cares, and its fray.

I shuddered to see, in the valley below,
My old forms of sorrow, and anguish, and woe,
My face pinched with pain, my pining regret,—
Nor knew they were mine.   I wept now to see
What trials for mortals on earth there could be.
I shrank from the scene, so sickening and sad,
Giving thanks that for me no such fate could be had.

I woke.   Youth had fled : again I was old ;
Youthful ardor had vanished ; the world again cold ;
Old memories revived ; I could not forget.
That vision of dreamland in my heart lingers yet.

Hades.

♣

WHERE are my hours of anguish ?
    And where those nights of tears ?
I know they rest and languish
    Among the sleeping years ;
But anguish knows no sleeping,
    A living presence, he.
The pain that caused my weeping
    Will know eternity.
There anguish all unspoken
    Will echo through the hours.
Remorse of one, heartbroken,
    Will smite his heaven's flowers.

Nature's At-one-ment.

OH, Thou Eternal Soul!
Thou gav'st me to know
The secret in the blade of grass,
And in the little flower : —
That they are one with Thee, and I with them.
And, knowing, feel the throbs in the pulsing tide
Of the secret of the universe.

*   *   *   *   *

The garrulous ocean knows, and babbling tells it well,
But better in its undertone,
When the tempest tortures to wrath the seething waves ;
Then louder the trembling secret swells,
And the eager listener falls upon his knees,
Deluged by a fervid torrent, which he knows
Is the pulsing current strong
Flowing throughout all Nature's unity.

45

Youth.

GO, youth! I know you may not linger
  Along the pathway I must go.
Yes, go! You take my precious jewels;
  But whither! Who can know!

I must sail on, and on, alway,
  Upon life's stormy main.
You backward sail, like yesterday.
  I ne'er sail back again.

And you will be as ship that passed
  And vanished in the night;
But memory long thy wake will cast
  Its phosphorescent light.

Then shall we never meet again?
  Forgotten mine and me?
Ah! Thou art mine, and such remain,
  Through all eternity!

In mighty vastness of the yonder
  Shall we united be?
Or will each seek "his own," I wonder,
  And seek eternally?

Night.

♣

CLOUDS press their lips to the crimson cheek of the western sky.
The twilight twines her tresses with locks of ebon dye.
The soft breeze sobs and whispers with melancholy sound.
The night has stars for the sky, but gloom for the dewy ground.

Dawn.

♣

THE tops of the mountains are held to the dawn's pink lips.
  Day pins to the sky her canopy folds of light.
Through the coral and lace of the peppers a golden sunbeam drips.
And clouds heavily lean 'gainst the shut gates of night.

47

Time's Tillage of the Heart.

I

TIME has shorn my heart's garden as barren of leaves
 As a meadow is after the mowing.
I confide all my sighs to the care of the breeze
 Which over the stubble is blowing.

II

Time now turns in my heart furrows long and so deep,
 And subsoils the fresh bleeding trenches,
Unheeding my cries, or the tears which I weep.
 Has pity grown cold in the heart of his henches?

Why harrow my torn heart again and again?
 And tread it with feet roughly shodden?
Oh! Feel you no anguish, or throes of my pain?
 Or my quivering, each step you have trodden?

III

My heart's fallow is broken.   Time's plowing is done.
 His henches are all idly waiting

What seed I shall scatter, or if there be none,
 And all to the briars and brambles forsaking.

Shall my sowing be tares?   Oh, my cost was too great !
 Then shall there be thistles a-growing ?
Or shall I have weeds ?   They bloom early and late.
 No !   The harvest will liken the sowing.

Would the wayfarer smile at my garden of leaves,
 Though no leaves were kept brighter or greener ;—
As he will, if my harvest has low bending sheaves,
 With the scattering ears for the gleaner ?

Oh, why will we moan, when the husbandman Time
 Tills our heart, that the seed we may scatter !
When he harrows our heart, we need not repine,
 Neither call his heart tillage disaster.

Fancied Bondage.

♣

WHY, through the live-long night, oh, sea!
　Thy moaning murmurs fill the air?
Thou art not fettered! Thou art free!
　And free winds toss thy hoary hair.

Ah, me! And it is thus through life:
　We pace like caged gazelle,—
Pace back and fore, in madd'ning strife.
　If tethered, we cannot tell.

Will restless souls on the other shore
　Resume their weary march again,
As if their bonds were taut and sore,
　And freedom theirs to gain?

Midnight.

♣

'TIS night, and the sky's bending meadow blazes
　With stars strewing over like ox-eye daisies.
The clouds' woven haze seems like heavenly highlands,
Or borders of palms on far distant islands.

Thy Will Be Done.

CROSS the sky a veil is stretched, and voices cry,
If I must sink in death, I must know why !
And not a word upon the mystic veil is writ,
And nothing on the green earth under it.

But unseen fingers turn unseen leaves for me;
I read a page I cannot even see.
A message hovers near, and yet no sound I hear;
Its touch is like my shadow hovering near.
I neither see, nor hear, nor know;—yet sure am I
Death is our Father's gift.   So let me die!

It is His light, that comes from far-off heights to me,
Which penetrates the distant veil I see,
And falls in unseen mists of sanctifying rain,
And tells me o'er and o'er, to die is gain.

My Own Shall Come to Me.

✦

ALL other gifts shall come
    Clustering to love and purity.
If prayer of lips be dumb,
    Prayer in the heart is security.

No one can lift from me
    Unalterable fate's fraternity :
My own shall come to me,
    And bide through all eternity.

Each dewdrop knows its own,
    Cherishing its nightly destiny,
As Autumn sheaves what seed was sown,
    Or bees the flowers' expectancy.

I Want to Know.

♣

ARE clouds the cast-off robes of the storm?
  Is day the child of the sun?
Is night a kin to the evening star?
  And the moon a bastard one?

Are seas the tides the Infinite weared
  Where the sunset laves its light?
Are mountains hands which the earth has reared
  In prayer all these days and nights?

Is snow spray-drift from the airy tide,
  And earth its ocean strand?
Is moonlight's sheen aerial veils
  Cast o'er the dreaming land?

Is noontime's flush the purpling showers
  O'er the sunset's bosom strown?
Is June's perfume the souls of the flowers
  As each one seeks its own?

Is Nature Depraved?

DOES the little world of the lily keep
  A record of the flowers
It so proudly laid at the Summer's feet,
  The sultry Summer hours ?

Does the violet hide, by its little heart,
  A lease upon the snow ?
Or the roses teach ev'ry thorn its smart,
  And tell them where to grow ?

Does the breeze from the laugh of the ocean write
  Those billows' cursèd notes,
That the angry wind, some tempestuous night,
  May wreck the sailors' boats ?

Each Waits Its Own.

THE flow'ret waits the coming bee ;
  The shore the waves caress.
  Then wait, your own shall come and be
  A curse or blessedness.

54

Delayed Spring.

♣

'TIS May ; but the peaks of the mountains are pale,
And torn by the wrath of a recent gale.
In pity for the rended and storm-trampled vale,
    They plead for the spring-loving lilies.
With cheek to the cheek of the wintry storm,
They tell of their hopes for the babies unborn,
    The dear little daffy-down-dillies.

    *   *   *   *

One more of Boreas' storm-loving kin,
In his icy sepulcher is gathered in,
And one more winter is the what-has-been :
    And flowers in the valleys are growing.
The peaks of the mountains keep watch in the sky,
Lay their cheeks to the cheeks of the clouds passing by ;
    What they say but the raindrops are knowing.

My Little Book.

THOU photo of my inner life
  (Not wholly, but in part),—
Go, little book, in love, not strife,
  Nor master poet's art.
Go ! Seek the friends, whose love invites
  Thy touch, from heart to heart.

Perhaps some little, little rhyme,
  Some hearth may linger nigh,
And some old friend, at evening time,
  May read, with failing eye,—
And hear, like half-forgotten chime,
  A voice he knows is I.

C

www.ingramcontent.com/pod-product-compliance
Lightning Source LLC
Chambersburg PA
CBHW030716110426
42739CB00030B/628